DID YOU PUT THE WEASELS OUT?

In Praise Of Weasels

'If you want elegant prose and earnest exhortations, sadly you have come to the wrong place.'
Floyd Sprouse

'An oddball collection that staggers through the fringes. I'm still not sure why it was sent to me.'
Dr. Kenneth Grogan,
Remote Sensing Specialist, PhD in Earth Observation

'I am not endorsing this. It has nothing to do with wind turbines.'
Jack Brett,
Ecopower Developments

Did You Put The Weasels Out?

Niall Bourke

A Perverse Novel In Verse

 EYEWEAR PUBLISHING

And Sétanta did hammer-puck the sliotar with his hurl
and it did fly down the hound's gullet like a weasel down a drainpipe
and the hound did drop dead with a mighty *eeek*.
'Oh my hound,' did say Culann, *'you have ball-fucked...*

First published in 2018
by Eyewear Publishing Ltd
Suite 333, 19-21 Crawford Street
Marylebone, London W1H 1PJ
United Kingdom

Cover design and typeset by Edwin Smet
Author photograph by Niall Bourke

Printed in England by TJ International Ltd, Padstow, Cornwall

The right of Niall Bourke to be identified as author of
this work has been asserted in accordance with section 77
of the Copyright, Designs and Patents Act 1988
ISBN 978-1-912477-12-8

WWW.EYEWEARPUBLISHING.COM

... my hop-happy hound and who is it that will now shite on my carpet?
Who is it that will scratch all the paint from my doors and eat all my post
but never the bills?' 'It will be me,' did say Sétanta,
'I will be your hound,' and so it was that Sétanta became the hound of Culann.

For Orla
and Nadine

Niall Bourke
graduated from Goldsmith's
Writer/Teacher MA in 2015 (with distinction)
and since then has been published widely in a number
of journals and magazines in the UK and Ireland.
He writes both poetry and prose and has been
longlisted for *The Short Story Award* and shortlisted
for *The Over The Edge New Writer Of The
Year Award* (2015, 2016 and 2017), *The Bare
Fiction Poetry Prize, The Costa Short Story Award,
The Cambridge International Short Story Prize* and
The Melita Hume Poetry Prize for best first collection
for a poet under 35. In 2017 he was one of
twelve poets selected for Poetry
Ireland's *Introductions Series*.
This is his debut collection.

TABLE OF CONTENTS

Contents

1 A Freudian haunting from the viscera
of Mark's childhood, as will become clearer.

2 Gaelic: it translates as 'the pre-stories' or, less literally, 'the stories of the minor appendages'. In *The Táin* they function as prologues, but here the author uses them more as appendices.

Part The First
The Pillow-Talk

I.

Goethe[3] writes: '*Be bold, and mighty*
Forces will soon attend your aid.'
It runs in Latin too, more tightly:
Carpe Diem. Both solid and staid
Maxims – to pull up your collar,
Clamp down fedora[4] tight and saunter
Outside to face down the drawls
And unsure roars of future squalls.
But just how apt is this advice
To jam a foot inside the door
Of chance? Or should we ignore
It as dangerous (if concise)
Nonsense? A man towels his chin.
And it's here, dear reader, we'll begin.

3 This phrase is actually attributed in relation
to Canadian clerical sensation, Basil King.
But Goethe is better suited to Mark's literary bent,
which will be revealed (to some extent).
The modern teen is more familiar, it would seem,
with this Latin sentiment of adventure as 'YOLO'
(so often shouted when striking out, like Marco Polo,
on their gap years). And so, reader dear, Goethe
(or Basil King – if that's your thing)
is reduced to curious (and pseudo-spurious) acronym.
How the purist's head must spin.

4 This hat, as we will see, is not as innocent or esteemed as it seems.

II.

Let us make a start with a sleepy
Chap[5] descending the stairs like a cube
Of toothache. Jenny, with a creaky
Yawn, is waking up in a mood.
'She scoffed the last slices,'[6]
(Thinks Mark – aghast.) *'When home from Isy's*
Bloody engagement completely soused,
Clumping around the fucking house
As if she'd brought home some atrocious
Rhino from that safari-park
Of a party, tearing apart
The kitchen like a fucking stocious
Dervish!' Jen descends. The stairs creak.
The gaping breadbin, grave-mouth bleak.

5 His name is Mark Setanta. He was a precocious young
bright-spark from Ballinteer
who read beyond his years. He now lives in a shrunken Archway
flat with his fiancé. He studied Geography at university
before two years doing a post-grad in Business Law.
And, to complete the jigsaw,
it is worth getting the following out in the open:
his oaty breakfast resolve has broken.
That is: he usually eats porridge but, and without warning,
has decided to have toast this morning...

6 ...But there is no bread!
Jenny ate it in the dead of night,
after pouring in like a mid-night wight.

LORD KNOWS I CAN BE CRUEL

And that morning, the type of morning
for putting the neighbour's post in the bin
when you'd ate the last heel of bread,
I chose my words, whetting them
so they came out edged. I chose them
so they slotted out flat and cornered,
like the tray under the toaster that collects the crumbs.
And I delivered them
in between your fourth and fifth ribs
like I was sliding in that rusty fucking crumb-tray
to collect the little croutons of your heart.
Christ, we weren't even fighting.

III.

Glazed over,[7] absently gazing,
Sitting, suited, fixing his tie
A patterned kitchen curtain making
Faces through half-moled eyes,
Whispering mouths spitting out spears
Which lance Mark's blistering ears.
'That tie,' they sigh, *'will hang you tight*
So wield instead a naked knife;
Take off that shirt and burn your clothing.
Be done with work, be rid of stress,
And say 'Get fucked!' to formal dress,
Go live a life of naked roving –'
The tick-tocking clock shocks Mark free.
The voice dies off, the moment flees.

7 Jen has left,* slamming the door so hard it clinks
the stained-glass panes. Left by the sink,
Mark tries to eschew the spiteful battle which ensued. **

* Reader - if we draw back time's black-out blind
we see that Jenny, who came in half-blind-tipsy,
did not molest the bread at all
but (after a clumsy fall) instead mistakenly
tidied it alongside her late-night whisky
bottle. Mark, on finding this lurking, crusty ghost,
has self-flagellated by burning his toast
(to shit), and is now chewing mournfully at the kitchen table.

**His exact words were:

'What gives? Seneca would laugh out loud to see me now so cowed, kow-towed and bowed
down so low before the lack of any ready bread.' Precocious? He's off his head.

IV.

Bank station, and stuck. Mark recalling
A book on how time's cold blade
Is honed: *'Each stroke a marauding*
Assault against the palisade
Of order, the sword of Damocles
Descending through the galaxies.'[8]
On the tube, an oxter becomes his muse:
'Why, it's all an elaborate ruse –
Fake, dreamed up, simply invented
(Seconds dictated by the rate
Caesium atoms dissipate[9]*)*
So that appointments are frequented
And meetings fixed. A con,' he smirks,
'To make us timid brides to work.'

8 This must be from all the Seneca he reads.
Or maybe the Bede.

9 For further information please see:
The New Quantum: Explorations On Caesium Atomic Decay.
But, to allay any fears, it appears
that Mark has not actually read this himself.
You may also want to get the following off the shelf:
Cú Chulainn and *The Táin* (an Irish, 8th century, epic narration
with which Mark has developed a recent fascination),
the tragic and astringent case of Joyce Carol Vincent,
Max Planck and Niels Bohr, Erwin Schrodinger (and his moggy)
and Pacific Prince Lee Boo's foggy arrival on these shores.

V.

'Elsewhere in the cosmos, perhaps,
Electron death is not so sure;
Jobs and work-days would collapse,
9 to 5's could not endure,
Dependent on what weird speedings
Atoms release their quantum seedlings.
Death to Chronos, whose scything hands
Control our lives!' Mark demands.
But, on arriving late for working,
He sees that here on earth the clock
Still roars a tyrannical *TOCK*
And mechanic *tick,* as, irking,
Red of face and unimpressed,
His boss[10] stands waiting, by his desk.

10 Mark works in mergers at Rockbarton, Rockbarton & Biers.
He has been with them for three years.
Now at this point it may be tempting – but remiss –
to dismiss his boss, Mike, as a simple asshole.
Mike is, in fact, a slightly more complex asshole.
Mike has recently been promoted
and believes he must so spread some bloated overcoat
of authority on his team in order to promote
his (honourable?) dream of keeping his family,
on whom he dotes, in a lifestyle with which they are clammily
familiar. He is still an asshole and a pain,
but only in the same way that the rain
is an asshole when the weather is dire
and, cycling home, you get a flat tyre.

VI.

'You're bloody late!' 'Sorry Mike. Tube delay.'
'Delays, my foot. Do you think we have
The money to just throw away
On slackers! Be on time – *or grab*
Your coat.' 'But the tube...' (pleading.)
'Stuff the tube!' Spat out like gleaming
Strafe of pellets. Mark ducks down.
'Now get yourself into that *Brown*
& Leverson meeting and complete
That acquisition!' Mark slopes off,
Nursing with salt-sulk a riposte
To the boss's tongue as he retreats
Along the shining, wooden floor.
Jill stops him by the boardroom door.

THAT I MAY KNOW YOU BY YOUR FINGERS

It was the orange Shellac of her lingering hand,
left light on my forearm when asking me for staples,
that made me think of *your* hand
and that open-curtained room percolated up
through the porous rocks of my memory,

the sodium spill of the street lamp breaking on your head,
(rested upon my chest so I but an out-house of your hair)
breaking like rust trickling from a tap
onto the inverted bowl of a blackened spoon,
and splaying onto your fingers,
fingers trying to coax me back to erection
not from any real desire I could now see,
but just to see if it was possible
so soon afterwards, to hold the warmhard fact of my feeling
in the palm of your ghostly orange hand.

'*Staples?*'

VII.

Jill gives up with a Mark-bemusing
Grin. He stares at the oaken door
Like a lonesome priest disabusing
Himself upon a basement floor
While on secret Thai vacation.
There is no time for vacillation.
If Mark doesn't get in there fast?
A shoe[11] inserted up his ass.
He reaches for the golden handle
But weasels of doubt slow-ascend
His spine. Some then spread out, befriend
His fingers. *'Become a very vandal*
To the grey walls of your career,'
Say the mustelids in his ear...

11 It is the sole of Mike's Size 7 loafer
that threatens to chauffeur
Mark's hole (into unemployment).

VIII.

'Why did you leave old Dublin city?[12]
Was it to choke on swallowed bile,
And wallow in your own self-pity,
You left behind the Emerald Isle?'
He stops. What was it that mattered
When he was younger?[13] What scattered
dreams (that now lie strewn like stones)
were carried forth when leaving home?
He works hard, earns good wages,
has good friends *and* pays his tax
(his hand now pressing down the latch)
he is honest, he is courageous
sometimes, loves his (de-facto)[14] wife.
What more should one dare ask from life?

12 See *'Some Denizens'*.
13 See *'The Chant'* – where Mark remembers the whoops of his boisterous boyhood troop.
14 The date has been set for the 17th July; a moderate affair but will rely on Titanic amounts of bougainvillea, a harpsichord and a flautist - called Ophelia.

AN IRISH ACTUARY FORESEES HIS DEATH

My father read me a story once. It was about a warp-spasm warrior called Cú Chulainn, who saved the sons of Ulster from the amassing armies of Connaught. For months, he fought them in fords of rivers, one man at a time, not stopping for eating nor sleeping, until the mounds of bodies swelled up so high that the streams of Ulster became more meat than water.

Eventually he was injured beyond standing.

To hide this from the Connaught men, he lashed himself, using shackles hacked out from his own hair, to a stone at the maw of a crossing. There he died, still staring down his mourning enemies through the mountains of their dead. The Connaught army dared not pass. Not a man of them. Not for a whole week. Not until the wheeling ravens came down and tattooed out his death with their talons. Ulster was saved. The crows clawed out Cú Chulainn's eyes.

That's how I'll go too. I'll die slaying an army.

I'll turn and face the massed ranks of drudges that have dragged in my wake, heap-piling high their average carcasses into massacre-mounds and then, when I'm whey-faced and spent and pinioned with darkling wings circling in blackening waitwheels, I'll bind myself to the final rock of my resistance and wait for the birds to hero-feast on my face.

But not today. Today the sky is too blue for fighting.

Today I can see no gyring ravens. Today I like my face too much.

So today Cú Chulainn can keep the ardours of Ulster, and I'll keep my eyes where they are. Sleeping on sound deep and down in their sockets.

SOME DENIZENS[15]

Asterix, called Asterix because of her uncanny resemblance to Asterix (moccasins, t-shirt, bottle of potion), her mate, Obelix, who looks nothing like Obelix but sure what the fuck else would she be called, the lad with the ferret on the sparkly lead who always buys four Carling and a six-pack of rashers,[16] that degenerate Toes who drank himself legless the night he fell asleep in his own bonfire and the shins only burnt *claane* offa him, his total spunksprout of a father who turfed Toes out on the street after the sixth time he'd pissed the stairs while trying to crawl to the jacks, your wan who lived only on cider and porridge for a whole year and contracted the first case of scurvy since 1837, that chap with the wife who looks a bit like a curtain, the poor auld Sniper's Nightmare who got polio when he was little and now zig-zags up the street, that quarehawk who sits on the wicker chair in the sweet shop muttering *did you put the weasels out?* (depending on what story you listen to she either: a) was a prostitute, b) keeps a hammer in her bag, c) killed a prostitute with a hammer, d) became a prostitute so she could afford to start a hammer collection), the topless lad who just kind of appeared one weekend and with the wife-beater only scalded onto him, Goonie, The Firebug Brennan, The Firebug's daughter (dances a bit like a pigeon), The Wolf when he got fined for all the howling, Fritz, Granite Head throwing the stones, Nadger and Shambles, Stabby Brophy and the eyes on her like murderous floodlights when roaming into ceremonies to ask for change, Scarecrow always baytin' the heads off the birds, your wan that died cycling home but into a cow,

---

15 He has now remembered why he left home...
16 An ex-monk called Ultan – Remscéal I.

The Spike, who – on the last Sunday of every month (and to the delight of the assembled patronage) – bombs it down the hill outside McCarthy's dressed as an eel and with the dog only going daft in the basket, The Sow,[17] The One Eyed Whistler, Up Up Umbrella, whatever fucking louse that keeps stealing everyone's jackets, all the above in one house party to end all house parties, some of the above cathartically sprinkled, none of the above – all of us poorer.

17 And Lushy, his partner in crime, who will both turn up again from time to time.

THE CHANT [18]

He got the scars, the story went,
when his mother (not paid the rent)
went out drinking for the night
and forgot she left the hob alight.

His milk, simmering in the pan,
abseiled upward, overran the edge.
John-Joe heard the blackening hiss,
tottered in – reached – missed.

Reached up above again. The milk rained down
in spears. Melted off both his ears. After lunch
we'd pick our sticks, (thick, hard),
and then chase John-Joe round the yard,

singing (thicker, harder still)
John-Joe, John-Joe,
your Mam's Dis-Grace,
with just one arm

and half your face.

18 ...and now has remembered what mattered when he was younger.
Why does he plunder his memories so?

IX.

But did life used to be more joyous?
Music that Mark had long forgot,
Today drowned by other noises
(*The Doors* and *Bowie*, smoking pot
As he gasped and gaped, astounded,
At *The Velvet Underground and
Nico)* return. Lately? Consorts
With his team, performance reports
And contorted spreadsheets fill his hours.
He used to read by bedside desk
The Golden Gate by Vikram Seth.
Nowadays it is *The Powers
Of Management,* or some such tome[19]
He studies on arriving home.

19 Such as *Release Your Inner Bad:
How To Tap Those Fifty Skills You Never Knew You Already Had.*

X.

Entire weekends himself and Jenny
Squandered once, sweating supine
In their room while resisting any
Outside ingress. *'Oh, such sublime*
Hours of such high, languid idleness!'
But no time now for such excesses.
Inside that awful bored-room wait
PowerPoints about higher-rate
Tax, disbursement, depreciations,
Jibbering managers who speak
In buckling tongues. Knees creak
Beneath weight of abominations.
He turns away, and by degrees
Walks,
     then jogs,
          then runs.
               He's free.

DO YOU REQUIRE AN ADVICE SLIP?

Make time each week to let the word Schnubart
molest your tongue; about-to-unblock is better
than the unblocking; spend more time watching
ants; learn to skim stones; seek out nature
documentaries that do not anthropomorphise
their protagonists; despite some initial promise
there is, in fact, limited comic potential for substituting
the words Liberian and librarian; do the washing up
so badly that you will never be asked to do it again;
wear a cloak sometime; seek opportunities to use
the word roustabout; force a cold caller to hang up
on you; the look on your brother's face when his child
unwraps a trumpet you bought outweighs the cost;
the dimensions of toilet cubicles makes learning
the maracas a viable option while waiting in airports;
behold: the court sections of provincial newspapers;
the humming of a fridge can soften the sound of time
dripping down through the rafters, because that is
the why; lovingly lovingly; when out baiting badgers
ensure you put twigs down your britches for they won't release –
until they hear a snap.

Part The Second
The Rising Pangs

I.

The sun has left behind the morning
And sends on down a tepid braid
Through the bank of clouds, warming
The streets. People avoid the shade
That the buildings cast on Eastern
Footpaths. Some, having not yet eaten
Are looking for a coffee shop
To buy lattes or a croissant
Or ~~assuage~~ a sausage. But Mark transcended
Hunger when he eloped work,
Obtaining a Zen-filled, kirk-
On-a-mountain state of extended
Calm, a brief moment of ~~sausage~~ assuage[20]
Absconding from his office cage.

20 This apparent mistake of the author's should come as no surprise;
a sound surmise is a typographical spoonerism caused not just by similarity in spelling
but also because much of the earlier poem has been about people smelling
breakfast.

II.

Standing almost still, his chest heaves
And breathes in the city's scent.
What can this protest hope to achieve?
Misleading – that's not the intent.
Mark, simply, just cannot stay slaving
Inside, he must go stroke the paving
Stones of gnarled city streets
With unfettered soles of feet
And an unfettered soul, to
Taste, if just for today, the faces
Of ancient laneways, the carapaces
Of towers, to chew bridge-side views
And nibble everything he sees:
Buildings, buskers, parks and trees.[21]

21 Mark now rambles off like a day-dreaming guitarist's hand
in a Led Zeppelin tribute band, intent on ~~exorcising~~ exercising his demons.

MEANWHILE, IN OTHER NEWS

I
In a recruitment agency in Bethnal Green,
a Bavarian Troubadour (complete with tricorne)
signs a contract, with a dog-ended Biro. Here ends her life
of wandering minstrelsy.

II
Two thousand, five hundred and eighty-seven people
are having sex (mostly in pairs). If you could gather them all up
and deposit them inside some unfeasibly large animal carcass,
from a great height they might look like maggots.

III
A child in Harlesden looks at an antique
globe. *Antanarivo*, he says, *Addis Ababa,*
Parimaribo, Mbabane, Djibouti,
the word in his mouth like bees.

IV
In a Bermondsey café, a man reads about a woman
who lay undiscovered in her apartment for five years.
He stops mid-article, in exactly the way your dog never will
when it is riding your Auntie's leg. Is this incontrovertible
proof of the city's moral decline, he wonders? Or simple
reaffirmation of an earlier suspicion: that it's very hard
to stop people intent on reducing themselves to curd.

V

In Kilburn, a teacher has written *'feedback'* on the board
but the *d* and *b* resemble a penis and testicles.
Laughter lakes the room. Anger slips its sack,
and ascends through her depths bloated and pale.

VI

A biology student in New Cross lies on her bed
pretending to study. She is really half-heartedly
masturbating to a cross-sectioned diagram
of the reproductive system. She comes
and can't shake the feeling she's lost her last fiver
and then found the keys.

VII

On a bench by the Thames
he watches a boat
carve out silver runnels
like an old Russian miner.[22]

22 Before heading direct to Hampstead, Mark instead
follows the river past Shad Thames down to Rotherhithe.
 He arrives, (after first stopping in *The Mayflower*
for an hour) at the lone and dusty tombstone
of Pacific Prince Lee Boo, now buried far from home.
Prince Lee Boo was from Palau's shores
and came to Rotherhithe in 1784.
A British ship, *The Antelope*, was wrecked, devoid of hope,
on a remote Pacific island. The natives, for a meagre stipend,
helped the crew repair and mend the boat and, once done,
Lee Boo accompanied them to London
where he became the talk of the town
and, dressed in hat and gown, attended many a fashionable party
and gathering of the rich and arty. But Lee contracted the pox
and ended up in a box. The heart bleeds
at the epitaph on his grave, which reads;
Stop reader, stop! let Nature claim a tear –
a Prince of mine, Lee Boo, lies buried here.

III.

1666: Conflagration
Terribilus devours London town.
Poor Saint Paul's – incineration –
13,000 homes burn down.
Monument, a tall memorial
To passers-by, a tutorial
That in Pudding Lane a baker
Razed it all to ash and crater.
62 metres high.[23] Mark attacks
The 311
Spiralling steps like seven
Accountants saving Starbuck's tax.
The top. Stops. Drinks in the bends
And pewtered passings of the Thames.

Lee Boo's Last Words
To think they thought I'd eat them!
But I'm fire-tired now, dragged down and bedded,
and my closing lids draw up sunrise wedded water,
sound swaying slow swashbackwash of sea I'll no more see.
To think they thought I'd eat them, I fear they've eaten me.

23 This all seems to check out. But bread? Causing all this trouble again? I dread
what lies ahead.

IV.

Gulls that swoop and dive like Stuka
Between pillars of Tower Bridge
And see, circling, the feluccas,
Trawlers, tugs that zig like midges
Down below, 'twixt catamarans
And passenger-boats, understand
That from such advantaged eye
The city is of course alive:
Roads are clogged-up arteries,
The river is a crooked spine,
Iron-skeleton railway lines
Support the asphalt capillaries
Transporting the sustaining swells
Of biogenic human cells.[24]

24 Here Mark too from this lofty eyrie
sees anew the liquid vein
pulsing lifeblood 'neath the dreary
cloud, and ponders with sticky pain
on themes that surface from below in
gulps – a chartered Thames; flowing
constrained, forced to defray
the city's ostentations like a stray
King's toxic urethra, muscling
out rippled knolls and silent folds,
lapping up against shoals
of lunch-hour folk and bustling
tourists, who both caw and coo
(as happy folk are wont to do).

RIVER RETIREMENT BLUES

I used to be a beast of burden. I flooded warehouses from brim to brim
Boats sat rank on rank, packed in so tight that men could plank
Across from bank to bank, humping hods and railroad rods
Without fear of falling in. I used to be the working river,
A Thor of ebb and tide. I floated folk, and carried smoking coke
Until the city choked on smelting lead and pig-ironed piles,
Lashed down tight with rigging-rope. I grew this city wide.
I used to flaunt my flowing muscles,
Feel envious eyes agog as my liquid limbs
Sole sustained the ravenous cranes, stretched
And strained, always loading to the never-closing
Thames docks drowned in fog.
Now? I am a dreadnought at the breakers,
A shackled Kraken chained and tamed.
Now? I flowly slow; sulking, soporific,
As tourists (thinking it terrific)
Take holiday snaps from upon the back
Of some toothless tiger leashed and lamed.
I was a working river.
Liquescent envy of the world.
But, weakly now,
My weary smiles
Meanders meek
The many miles
And I,
A neutered tomcat, lie
Sleeping round
The city curled.

Part The Third
Hand-to-Hand Combat

A FORMER GEOLOGIST'S UMBRAGE UPON SEEING A TRAMP [25]

You can't just couch on the pavement like a glacier
and the moraine of your yellow meltwater
circling the dark outwash plain of your silt.
Because it's here, under the weight of your rivulets,
that I become that bouncer again, the drunk one
patting himself down for contraband erections
outside the we-both-know-you're-not-getting-a-note nightclub.
But you do seem to like the cirques of meths
that catch between the arêtes of your blanket,
so who am I
to halt the valleys you're carving in the ground?
Ah here, have the fucking pound.

25 This ne'er do well is a disgraced and (now rabid) Abbot
who has taken to wearing some unsavoury habits
of late – see Remscéal I when done.

I.

Hampstead Heath.[26] The city's shining towers
On the horizon, through the haze,
Hemming the heath like silver flowers.
But Mark is not looking, his gaze
Instead is with the children flying
Kites, each a patchwork clown decrying
The morning's car doors falling off,
Throwing custard pies at his boss
And honking noses, the Size Fifteen
Shoes of his clumsy words to Jen
Trip over themselves, again
And again in his mind, umpteen
Jesters tracing out coloured trails
With lazy wavings of their tails.

26 The original house of one John Keats
where he wrote his most famous work
backs up onto Hampstead Heath
his artistic grotto once he'd shirked
a brief foray into surgeoning
to concentrate on his burgeoning
poetry. 'Bright Star', 'La Belle Dame
Sans Merci', his 'Odes', 'To Autumn'
– works of unparalleled brilliance
that no one actually read
until *John K.* was long cold dead.
Such principle and resilience –
But not a pot to piss in; poor
and dead on turning 24.*

* Keats, of course, died aged 25. What belies
such authorial besmirch given all the earlier research?

ECONOMIC DEVELOPMENT[27]

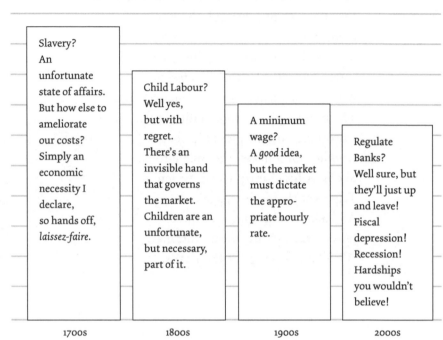

Arguments used by the rich when silly peopeple with no undestanding of how the economy works propose curbing practices which allow rich people to make themselves even richer (thinks Mark)

Slavery?
An
unfortunate
state of affairs.
But how else to
ameliorate
our costs?
Simply an
economic
necessity I
declare,
so hands off,
laissez-faire.

Child Labour?
Well yes,
but with
regret.
There's an
invisible hand
that governs
the market.
Children are an
unfortunate,
but necessary,
part of it.

A minimum
wage?
A *good* idea,
but the market
must dictate
the appro-
priate hourly
rate.

Regulate
Banks?
Well sure, but
they'll just up
and leave!
Fiscal
depression!
Recession!
Hardships
you wouldn't
believe!

1700s   1800s   1900s   2000s

Time

27 'The city's shining towers... hemming the heath like silver flowers...'

II.

'How many hats have I now rested
On my head? A Cap I doff
And wring toadily when molested
Across the desk by Mike and Ross,[28]
A Stetson of solid fortitude
For the in-laws, a multitude
When with Jen: a Baby's Tam
For cooing nothings during jam
Dark nights, childish Chapeaus for goading
Fights; when flushing with swells of lust
A Crown of Crimson that combusts
(Before cooling and then eroding
Away), a Beanie of the Young
When meeting with my Dad and Mum.[29]

28 Mark's immediate line
manager. A real remedial swine.

29 Why is Mark now muttering about hats? Well:
1) he's gone a bit bat-shit crazy
2) he's still pissed about that Pakol
that blew away in in Peshawar. And why the clown?
Don't ask about his dressing gown!*

*There is, of course, another theory.
That the author is a leery-
eyed hat lothario. Remember that fedora?
Well now it has lost its aura
of innocence – more Sodom and Gomorrah!

MY FATHER THE FOREST[30]

Someone is chopping up my father.
Bough by bough, limb by limb, knot
by knot, reducing him to kindling.
Someone is chopping up my father.

These days I often hear some scything
woodsman's thwacking, his relentless
whacking as his cowl and cape creep near,
and if I could find him I would kill him
but I cannot. So I watch my father rot.

In my youth my father was a mighty wood.
Hard to see it now, but he spread
out a huge canopy overhead, filtering light in just
the right amount until, through his branches, I climbed out.

Now he's been all but hacked right back
by some hourglass-wielding lumberjack
but he was a mighty forest once, I'll attest.
And as that tangled forest I'll love him best.

30 The narrative's mention of his Dad causes Mark to fear
things he has been trying hard not to hear.

III.

'And I have my own of course, neatly
Nestled near the stairs for when
I am alone and can discreetly
Take it out, dust it down and then
Put it on and so become myself.'
But lately, that musty, mothy shelf
Mark keeps behind a secret blind
Is strangely empty. He can't find
It. *'Don't be so daft,'* A soft rebuke.
'It'll turn up.'[31] The cool March wind
Carries things of which the city sings;
Of jostling markets, hidden souks,
Taverns, museums on a barge,
Exhibitions free of charge.[32]

31 Mark's heartaches
now begin to ~~Fez~~ fizz away
and he turns his meditations
out toward the metropolis;
burying his snood of irritation
like a votive outside the Acropolis.

32 In a rather odd turn of events,
the poem itself, having growing discontent
with Mark's more maudlin introspections,
has decided to interject and re-direct proceedings
in an address in the voice of Friedrich Engels
(who will appear again with some homesick Bengals).

Death And Taxes

I *heard* that communism was dead
in my history class,
it was called an 'anachronism'
which I looked up. It meant
'belonging to times now passed'.

But I *knew* that communism was dead
when I went to Highgate Cemetery Park
and they charged me
a four pound entrance fee
to see the tombstone of Karl Marx.

41

PAEDORISTS AND TERRORPHILES

Dog[33] in the park, barking and larking and haring around,
do you not know that we've had it? That the world
is warming up? That the economy is cooling down?
That paedorists and terrorphiles have invaded your attic?
That it's appalling, in times like these, with the GDP,
DOA and base interest rates falling fast, with lounging
dole-scroungers pounding us to our knees,
to bark at butterflies and wipe your hole on the grass?
So, my long-eared friend, act now, or you'll regret
(but too late I say, and to no avail!) your days
spent haring about in the park, larking and barking
and chasing your tail.

33 Leaving Hampstead, Mark steps in a wet-noodle
of dog shit and proceeds to unload on the next poor poodle
he sees.

Part The Third And A Half
Jen Battles the Morrígan

I.

Over at the British Library
Jen (who works as a ~~cure hater~~[34] curator)
Is dying slowly. Her fiery
Hangover will not abate, her
Fowl headache pecking out and clucking
Fuckityfuckityfuckfuckfucking
Hell. By coincidence,[35] Jenny too
Is reading about Prince Lee Boo
(Or trying to read, because Isy,
Not yet sober from the night before
Is being a manic, yammering bore
And babbling in Jenny's spicy
Ears like the proverbial brook
(Of effluent gobbledygook).

34 It is unclear the intention here – hair of the dog?

35 Jenny, with some serendiption,
has spent the last four weeks working on an exhibition
about the impact of Polynesian migration on Britain.
She has, just this very morning would you believe – no joke –
been bequeathed the original ship's anchor rope
and the Captain's log from *The Antelope*.

II.

'…And she threw her head back and guffawed
Like she was swallowing a pie!
At first I thought she was appalled
But then I realised why:
*Because **I** thought she'd said '**pissed**'*
*(But what she'd **really** said was '**kissed**')*
And so I'd said, 'Well, I was drunk
At mass one time and tried to hump
The vicar…' but kissed*? In Peru*
I did meet this gorgeous zither
Player…' – and so on, witter, witter.
Jen pretends she has work to do.
She really loves Isy, of course,
But cannot face her *tour-de-force*.

I AM A POLE[36]

but I have never met Lech Wałęsa. Nor did my mother,
a trade unionist at the canning factory in Katowice.
But I have drunk oily Wyborowa in the port city of Gdańsk
and thrown back my head to bite at the night
sky somewhere South of Poznań,
a sandy-haired mechanic licking the sweat from off my thighs.

I am a Pole. But now I live in a bedsit in Barnet.
I work the local fish shop. The manager is an arsehole.
Are you a flagpole? Or a barber's pole? he laughs
from among the hake and turbot.
I stand a fish into the floor. *Not my circus*
not my monkey, I dream of blue almonds.

I am a Pole. I should like Marie Curie
but I prefer Joanna Kuchta. I don't even like gołabki.
Last Christmas I pulled a slip of yellow hay
from under a white tablecloth so to see my husband.
I saw a strong-fingered fireman with an ass of iron.
Instead I got a dough-holed prick from Bognor.
I wish he'd leave for Liverpool like his brother.

I am a Pole. I have felt the wet of the Black Vistula
on a knickerless weekend up the Barnia Góra
as gallons of memories pooled in the wells of my feet.

46

36 Isy, her tongue still loosed by her engagement Gin, pours out to Jenny like a violin.
Jen pretends to read The Captain's journal. Isy finishes but then keeps babbling:
'And then there was that Colonel I met that time when I was travelling...'

JEN'S WILD NIGHT IN KENNING(TON)

I Bladder-breaker
I Off button-obliterator
I Decorum-oubliette
I Scene-shedder
I Text-Typhoon
I Jacket-chameleon
I Night-stroker
I Kebab-carouser
I Step-penguin
I Key-clanger
I Landing-ornament
I Bed-heron
I Sex-considerer
I Fuck-forgetter
I Tar-dreamer
I Clock-garrotter
I Mouth-upholstry
I Mattress-barnacle
I Bruise-bemused
I Shower-slug
I Commute-crustacean
I Work-weed[37]

---

37 Eventually Isy leaves and Jen reads the extract from the Captain's log,
The white noise of her hangover crackles and sits like fog
 just below the surface of her interior monologue
and her thoughts cavort across the playground of her mind
like children leaving class once they find
that a teacher they thought was merely late
is not turning up, no matter how long they wait.

ALL CONUNDRUMS BETWEEN CURATORS LEAD TO BREXIT

Question: You are a kitten on a flight from Catalonia
to Kathmandu (via Qatar). Due to an unseasonable and ferocious
typhoon the plane crashes deep in an unspecified jungle
of some remote banana republic. Everyone on board
is killed, including your parents. You alone are left,
mewling through the furballs of the wreckage.
You are saved from certain death when you are found
by a hand of wild bananas and taken in as one of their own.
For the next fifteen years it is just you and your feral banana family,
alone in the jungle. You learn how to ripen, how to lie motionless
for months with a thirty-degree curve in your spine,
how to emit the silent howls of jungle fruit.
Sometime after your fifteenth birthday, a pounce of explorers,
both jaunty of monocle and ragged of whiskers, are mapping
the source of a long-lost river of milk and stumble upon you.
You are wearing only a leaf; your fur has given way to a waxy
cuticle and smooth ochre ridges. Instead of walking on all fours
you hang with ferocious stillness. When spoken to, you respond
with utter yellow. Tenderly, but with caution, you are severed
from the bunch (after being thoroughly checked for spiders) and brought
back home. You become a brief media sensation – but are then forgotten
and entrusted to a convent of wimple-eared nuns who begin the slow
and torturous process of catalytic conversion. After four years,
and despite intensive lessons, it becomes clear that you are a fruitless
endeavour. You still insist on ripping off your tortoiseshell
whenever possible. Your voice retains a distinctive amber tinge.
48   Although you can follow rudimentary instruction, speech has not
developed beyond caterwauling. The nuns ascribe you to working
the laundry, the one job you can do with a modicum of success
(and minimum of supervision, it seems cathartic somehow)
and you become catatonic as you help them fulfil lucrative contracts
for the cleaning of bed linen of local hotels. Now – are you an ex-pat
or an immigrant?

Part The Fourth
The Fight With Ferdiad

I.

Opposite Clapham North tube station
Squats a pub, *The Royal Oak*
A spit-and-sawdust. Renovation
Would be needed for the city folk,
It might improve the aesthetic
But would kill the charm. A prosthetic
Leg hangs upon the toilet door,
Pints are spilled upon the floor,
Faded, tatty posters adorning
Walls like the exclamation marks★
Thrown about when cars won't start,
But if you're looking for more absorbing
Decorations, look to the clientele,
Whose evening tidal ebb and swell...

★ Or Asterix★★
★★ Her again! That fucker Obelix can't be far away...

II.

...Dictates the rather nebulous
Appeal, the true off-kilter *weird*
Of drinkers; bricklayers, pendulous-
Breasted hen night types, strange beard-
Wearing barmen, rugby-supporting
Clapham staples, two men purporting
To be famous, a gap-toothed crone,
A drunken navvy who should be home,
Crusty ~~loaves~~ students discussing Engels,[38]
Pissed up Paddies,[39] a singing Scot,
A passport some tourist has forgot,
Two soused Serbs, three homesick Bengals.[40]
And the conversations are just
As varied. Some, the cuts and thrusts —

Jean Charles de Menezes
It was agreed unfortunate (but not unwise –
what with commuters being terrorised)
to shoot Jean Charles de Menezes
seven times, in the back and in the head,
on a well-stocked Stockwell tube.

On that well-stocked Stockwell tube
young Jean Charles lay down and oozed
out and over the passenger's shoes.
Two nights straight – then off the news.

38 The poem has now lapsed into a dream
while waiting for Mark to re-enter the stream
of the narrative, possibly prompted by Engels
being mentioned again or, maybe, because it
too once worked as an electrician
in Kennington.

39 There's Obelix, the sneaky bastard.
And she's on the lash with The Sow and Lushy Mac.
(Do see Remscéal II for more
on this pair of wild, drunken ~~boars~~ bores).

40 Told you. And crusty loaves? Seriously?

III.

– And merry wars of old companions,
The fate of Madeline McCann,
The pros of Japanese expansion
Under Hirohito, the plan
To raise, through tax, a hundred million
By the incumbent coalition,
Why men are bores, why women suck,
The best way to disengage a ruck
And maul, Chelsea bound for victory
And Arsenal set again for woe
(*So Arsene Wenger has to go!*)
A gambler's valedictory
Whoop as he recoups coin for gin
And amid all this Mark blows in.

IV.

In approximately five minutes
Mark will be ensconced, down
On a stool with a pint of Guinness,
Watching its tumultuous brown
Clouding settle to bands of blackish
Tar, but must first endure the happy
Drunk at the bar – you know the type,
Shafts of wit to him, wafts of shite
To everyone else, has been pretty
Much everywhere, it seems, and done
Everything too, sucks the fun
Out of conversation with shitty
Aplomb, mangling words like vermin.
He spots his Mark. Here comes the sermon.

Cú Chulainn, drunk to fuckbuggery, crawls into a cab
and begins bending the ear off the at-work driver
(an out-of-work brick layer) about a TV show
in which a politician claimed five thousand Euro
for office toilet roll. The driver's getting angry
because the Lonnergan twins (with the *two n's*, mind)
are lying on a square of carpet in the middle of the road
and baytin' the bells off of each other with hose pipes.
Again. After they get dragged home by the mammy
the driver tells Cú Chulainn that sure the banks
only have the country ruined, ruined, and, anyways,
didn't his *cousin* hear that the politician was forced to sniff
The Bishop's sandwiches when he was a child
(when the politician was a child that is, not The Bishop.
The Bishop was a child once too, of course,
he played the harpsichord with precocious talent
and lived in the house with the sun dial in the garden.
But that's another story). Rome caught wind
of his olfactory predilections and sent him off to Guatemala
where he was put in charge of making packed lunches
for the local primary school. Cú Chulainn laughs at this so hard
that the all-day breakfast roll he was eating spills down the seat.
The driver turfs him out – half for acting the maggot/
half because he vowed to never allow another French *bejaysus* loaf
in his car again after that bleedin' goal in Paris.
Cú Chulainn swears he's done with drinking and falls asleep
on your front lawn. In the morning either 1) your man
driving the trimmer doesn't see him and chops him up.
The grief is palpable. Or 2) Cú Chulainn wakes up
before the trimmer, but still too late for work,
and gets a fierce bollockin' off the husband. After a blazing

blue barney they fold into each other like ironing boards
because, deep down, they both know that sure the banks
only have the country ruined, ruined and, anyways,
how is anyone meant to make a living anymore at all.

41 For all eight pages of the old drunk's next homily,
which Mark luckily – and without bonhomie –
escapes, see Remscéal II.

V.

The pub hubbubs and Mark is engaging
In a slithering verbal hug
With a woman called Masefield, an ageing
Sea dog[42] who began with a shrug
Regarding the lamentable changes
In shipping,[43] but, thankfully, exchanges
More to Mark's interest began.
'Howsh can a woman and a man
Ever truly undershtand the world
The other inhabits?' Masefield
Slurs, spilling almost congealed
Stout down her chest and into the furls
Of her shirt. Mark doesn't debunk
Masefield, being a bit too drunk.[44]

42 Ferdiad Masefield. She joined the Navy in 1994. (Note: *The Women's Royal Naval Core*
was reformed at the beginning of the Second World War and at its peak, in 1942,
had 75,000 members. The service continued after the war too,
but was disbanded in 1993 when women were integrated fully
into the Royal Navy). In May 2012, Commander Sarah West
(a close friend of Masefield) became – no jest –
the first woman in the Navy's history to command a major war ship.
However, she was controversially sacked
for having an affair with a junior hack – a move which,
between you and me, cut Masefield rather deep (as we'll see).

43 Which started: *"Quinquireme of Nineveh from distant Ophir,*
rowing home to haven in sunny Palestine…"

44 I.e. Mark is more romantic than Masefield thinks.
He once wrote a letter to Jen that went like this:
'I ferret through your tunnels like some needy stoat,
through your guano runnels I nourish roachlike.
Like an extremophile, in thermal vents deep and Atlantic,
I'm sustained by the sulphurs of your soils.
And, as pedantics need apostrophe's, frantically; so you are to me.'

VI.

'Mark, you have a wife I s'pose?'
'Fiancé.' 'Then, you know how it
Goes. Starts off all perfume and roses
Grown in the black, composted shit
Compiled from the sickly diets
Of Rom Coms, and the awful, biased
Tripe of adverts. But not for long.
Soon it becomes a nasty strong-
In-the-arm to decide who falls
On top, and who below. But I think
Love can really be heard by clink
Of coloured balls in billiard halls.'
Mark sups. 'I'm not sure I follow.'
Masefield speaks — her voice is hollow.

SNOOKERED

The black ball
is the one you really want
but it is sultrily close to the cushion.
It can be heart-breaking to plant your feet
and square up for the shot
only to watch it
jam in the pocket.

Here lie the reds. Although needed
to continue a break, people
really prefer holing
something
else.
The pink. Worth
slightly less than the black
but an easier pot. The path
to the pocket is more direct
but not guaranteed.

The black is a long shot.
The pink difficult. The blue
is mid-table. The blue is a safer option.
Unless you take an easier pot
of lower value.

Yellow   Brown   Green

Interchangeable. Really used to provide an angle back down to pink or black.
But beware the dreaded double kiss. It will leave you stranded. Forever.

Down the wrong end of the table.

VII.

Reader, let's take this skiff of meaning
And push it far away from shore
Into deeper waters, wild, seeming
Dark and murky. Let's watch Mark oar
Tentatively about in circles,
Caught between the uncertain purples
Of the vast and dusk-covered sea
Of Masefield's words and the scree
Of the orange-light-studded coastline
Where he lives, ensconced with Jen.
The harbour's friendly – but then again
He knows it inside out, each incline
Valley, wood and glen. He takes stock
From sweetsoft beach to spiky rock-

VIII.

-Face and then, rowing round in clumsy
Arc, turns to face the pocket-dark
Tide, watches flotillas of hungry
Doubts streaming out towards the shark-
Speckled and most mysterious
Ocean edge where, with imperious
And great adventurous spirit,
They then plunge below the limit
Of the horizon. Their findings
Might be what? Happiness? Freedom?
A life of single bliss, once heathen
Fears are tied to altars with bindings
Of action? Or years of regret [45]
And staring back through sad lorgnettes?

45 Oh pornography on the internet, *your* acquaintance does he now regret.
Not only a most inaccurate tutor, but also a wrecker of three home computers.

I FIRST MET YOU[46] IN MY PHYSICS BOOK

and Newton must have balanced you
and Kepler's laws of planetary motion
described the movement of your body,
while your smell was thermodynamics
all of it really, but particularly the second bit,
the bit in the box on the bottom of page twelve
about my increasing disorder inside a closed system.
Even Max Planck himself could not have more
accurately calculated the size of my constant
on long evenings spent locked in my bedroom
grappling with both the being and nothing
of your cat.

46 They walked not knowing what to say.
Where shall we go? What shall we do? I don't know. Up to you.
Perhaps, if she can now recall it,
down the back of some quiet lane,
there was a low-slung red-bricked wall
(with faded yellow mortar lines)
buried deep behind a privet hedge
(or maybe behind some evergreen pines?)
and there they squeezed in-between, wading ankle-deep
through the faded wrappers of crisps and sweets.
He sat down, she smoothed her dark-green school skirt
then stumbled in among his legs, threw away her cigarette,
they kissed. Her mouth was wet, his eyes were open.
The empty packets spoke in rustles round their feet
as the evening died   staked out on the leaves
(or was it on the pines? Or was it on the trunks of trees?)
Everything that mattered then seemed hung
tight upon two straining tongues as twenty fingers swum
with frozen violence through that stucklimbed well of silence.

Part The Fifth
The Final Battle

I.

Masefield is, somewhat predictably,
Smashed by now and Mark has left
Her back in the pub (criminally
Drunk)[47] to sail himself home with deft
(If tipsy) navigation towards
The lighthouse flash that Jen affords.
But there are a few swells to climb
Yet. 1. Boozing since dinner time.
2. He may not have a job tomorrow[48]
3. He cannot, just now, locate
His wallet[49] (he is already on probate
For losing keys he'd borrowed).
4. It is quite late into the night
And no text sent since their fight.

47 In muted caves of her recalling,
wrapped up in leathered sprawls
of dark-webbed hands, roost appalling
Memory Bats. Across these ragged halls
tumble mutterings of some younger voices,
folding back from rocky cloisters,
distant whispered waves of words
rolling, rolling, repentant slurs,
 on which the bats first rise – then dropping,
shaking, shaking. To stave them off
she knocks back shots in fits and coughs,
steels herself by the bar, half propping
up, then pours down libations.
In liquid, a prayer for annihilation.

48 Although he doesn't know it,
Mark has earned some good credit
at work and his indiscretion will be 'shredded'.

49 It is in the pub, under the table.
He realises this and is able to go back,
dodging a by now paralytic Masefield and making the penultimate tube
without further boob.

MY LOVE IS THE WEEDS

It grows easy and everywhere on minimal minding.
It can root in rock, needing no helping hand,
and flourishes unknown by fences
and near dead stretches of land. You endlessly battle
it, you try to deny its inevitable march.
You think a garden should look such and such,
but my weed doesn't care. When faced with your chopping,
spraying, burning and worse, it remains much nonplussed,
refuses to accept its curse. My weed always finds a way,
never ceases to succeed. So refute it, dispute it or uproot
to your pleasing. But, like it or not, my love is the weeds.[50]

50 (This is the text that Mark *wanted* to send – what he actually sent was…)

THE WORD CIRCUS

Roll up, roll up!
The crowd, ten deep, coo and caw
as, fearlessly, and dripping derring-do,
my cracking whip and inverted chair
manoeuvre snapping word-lions
into impossible positions,
paw on head, ten high, teetering a little
but the tower staying solid
their ferocious resistance
broken by the force of my will.

I don my red jacket,
pull on my breeches,
twiddle the ends of my pencil
moustache and sit ready to write
a performance.
But facing the silent and sandy circus
ring of a blank screen I must admit the truth.
I am not a suave tamer of lions,
I am a herder of recalcitrant house cats.
And, top-hatted head in hands,
I
            M ust   w a t c h
T h   e
            m
S
        C   A   T
                T   E   R

II.

'Motherfucking predictive texting!'
Mark thrashing his mobile against
A tube station wall, the perplexing
Sight of justice being dispensed
To an obdurate electronical
By a suited and melancholical
Drunk – a thwarted attempt to send
A conciliatory text to Jen.[51]
A t(annoying) announcement
'There are delays upon the line,
Other services running fine.'
The muttering denouncements
Ghost the platform as Mark laments,[52]
Hoping Jen won't take offense.

51 *'Hey, just gone for food'* turning to *'gone for good'*.
Although perhaps still not so unlucky
as the time he sent her a message
saying he couldn't *'wait to kick your puppy'*.

52 His surlier hyperbole now due to the stout
(rather than Seneca or Keats' house).

III.

City Road. The night, not quite balmy,
But not so cool he needs his coat
(Maybe a beer jacket) and Mark calmly
Assessing how best to cross the moat
And bailey of his indiscretions.
Amber laughter from a session
At the local[53] spill out, wets the road.
'Another drink before it's closed?'
An errant thought. *'Let me just get fucking*
Home sometime tobloodynight.' He yawns,
Stretches out his arms. And then it dawns,
With two oddly empty palms jutting
Skyward, that he's forgotten the gift
He bought for Jen to bridge their rift.

53 *'The Docker's ~~First~~ Fist.'* Much nicer than the name ~~fist~~ first suggests.

UNEXPECTED ITEM IN THE BAGGING AREA[54]

you say and then blink at me and I try to fathom
the depths of its unexpectedness. It is as if I have

carried you in a submarine to an underwater lecture
on Egyptology and a middle-aged octopus, in a plum-coloured

blouse, has just tentacled to a slide of Tutankhamun, making
you realise (for the first time and at the age of twenty-seven)

that the word sarcophagus is not pronounced sarko-FAYgus
after all. I mean, if it were a rift in the space-time continuum

or some caged animal's sandpapering of nostalgia or, even,
a hitherto prudish lover shattering unannounced the last taboo

with a kumquat, well, then I could understand. But it is a bottle
of Prosecco. A green one, in a supermarket. With a wine section.

54 Please see Remscéal III for the 'riastradh'* Mark has narrowly avoided.

* *Riastradh*. Gaelic: literally *'the twisting'* or *'contortion'*. More commonly rendered as *'warp-spasm'*.

IV.

A set of keys plays noughts and crosses
(Transatlantic? Read: *'tic-tac-toe'*)
With the lock, eventually squashes
Its resistance and a door blows
Open to reveal the sepulchre
Of the hall. The potted hellebore[55]
Is narrowly avoided, a foot
Is stubbed (and then a fist put
Into mouth and knuckles bitten:
'Not again for bloody fuck's sake!
I'm moving that shagging bookcase
In the morning!') In the kitchen,
A note in Jenny's cursive script
Waits like a rat inside a crypt.

55 'Any of several plants of the genus *Helleborus*, of the buttercup family,
having basal leaves and clusters of flowers, especially
H. niger, the Christmas Rose' (*The World Plant Encyclopaedia.*).
It was an (unwanted) engagement gift from Jen's mother.

V.

'Mark – you're a goose. I got your message.
Time I think for another phone?
(Or maybe fingers? ☺) Ross Lessage
called – he's so nice! He said *'don't*
worry about today. Every
thing is fine' ??? Last night's reverie
has caught up with me – I'm wrecked,
so I'm gone to bed. I suspect
that you'll be late so won't wait until
you come in, I'm up at the crack
of dawn tomorrow. Freddie Mac
is out sick – again! Bloody uphill
struggle at that place – what next!
I love you honey XXX[56]

56 Jen has completely forgotten about the fight.
Or, more accurately, there never was a fight.
Jenny was much, much too hungover (and late,
hence the slammed door) to give any weight
to Mark warbling on about bread, agitated
and waving his hands with manic fervour. *
Mark celebrates by making a sandwich before going any further.

    * That is the thing about Mark: he's sorely neurotic,
    as Jenny (who has learned to spot it)
    knows well. Sometimes, Mark becomes despotic
    like when he goes into a bookshop
    and only sees all the books he'll never read.
    And why would this key point not be revealed
    until after Footnote 50?
    Just one more ~~shitty~~ shifty authorial over~~shite~~sight.

AND WHO WHAT WILL TAKE CARE OF YOU?

The open fridge is beeping, but not beeping
like an open fridge, it is more like a foul-mouthed,
reversing truck being interviewed before the watershed,
more like a cyborg having a fit under an airport scanner
and impromptu starts the microwave, so desperate
to answer some question not even asked – *oh, oh, I know,*
pick me, pick me, but, before you can respond,
the square kid with the dirty glass face chimes in –
too hot too cold too something – and then, when
the dishwasher pipes up with its falsetto
the swinging fridge door is now leading a symphony,
a symphony that has been written by a foot
when its sock has fallen down below its heel,
a symphony being played by enthusiastic
(but very chrome and angular) musicians,
ones who have only ever seen the concept of music,
and that after it has been shone through a prism,
so when the tumble dryer completes the quintet
and their crescendo breaks over you like every
cancelled bank card, well then you know, oh you know
for certain, that we are indeed so lucky
to all be watched over by machines of such loving grace.[57]

57 This is a phrase from Richard Brautigan.
 (who wrote *Sombrero Fallout!* Now, we know what the author thinks about hats.
 But why flout it again?)

HALF A TOMATO SOMETIME AFTER MIDNIGHT

Just under half a tomato, wrapped in cellophane
and lurking between the crème fraîche (cultivating
mould) and the olives, sums up the difference between us.

I, who after slicing his tomato into the optimal amount
for a sandwich (so as not to sog the bread),
wrap up the remainder so it can escape the same fate
as the hardening cheese.

You, who sees no point in the savings of halves,
devourer of whole tomatoes, eater of full tins of beans
and drinker of the ends of purée tubes.

Sandwiched between the light of the fridge
and the dark of the kitchen, I relish
the weight of your shadow being cast
by this odd-shaped remnant of a past lunch.

I unwrap the tomato and sink in my teeth.
Those gooey seed things dribble down my chin.

VI.

The clock's struck two and nothing stirring,
Not even the proverbial.
Fanbelt[58] is curled up and purring
Contented, passing loud, verbal
Seal on the hallway radiator
(Re-settled after Mark displaced her).
If we pan up along the stairs
We can now watch them, unawares,
Snuggling down under cotton seams.
Around the house, cooling lightbulbs clink
As outside orange streetlights wink
Against the night. Jen turns in her dreams.
'Did you put the weasels out?'
'I did,' says Mark, 'without a doubt.'

58 Their cat. So named because of the odd whining
sound she makes when pining for food.

VII.

And that's it. The shades of night tumble
Down and so our curtain drops
And who knows what happens next? Fumble
Forward far enough and it's a box.
In the ground. For both of them, rotting
In the earth of course. Before that? Yachting
The globe? Children? Solid careers?
Laughter? Tears? Mortgage arrears?
A new dog? An aged cat? Or maybe
None of this at all. Or maybe all.
It is impossible to call.
The night departs as a weighty
Alarm clock sounds. Two fates sealed
As a dark March morning is revealed.

The Remscéala[59]

59 And so begin
the tales of dire and
unquenched desires.

I. THE EXILE OF THE SONS OF UISLIU

The weasels have woke me and I am standing by the kitchen window again, the silence of the monastery sat sharp on the spines of the morning, and the kettle is tocking out its sombre Matin across the laminate counter while outside, punctuated by one single beading of condensed kettle spume, an opioid darkness obscures the garden yet I know it still

how, what in the daylight looks like a single green sheet of lawn is actually, when down on hand and knee, clearly a much poorer amalgamation of disparate clumpings (mostly rye grass and fescue but also the invasive islands of white clovers blown in from over the wall) so when the Abbot[60] stops me in the hall each afternoon and tells to me how well the grass is looking – for it is me alone who now tends the garden since Brother Fergus's arthritis got so bad – the whole lawn stands against me in admonishment

but an admonishment that is so nearly offset by the plumes of Spanish lavender now rioting under the south-facing fence, the fence itself trellised with white clematis petals, because each bee-soaked stalk of purple lavender-ear sat atop an oval flower head sat atop again a thin down of peppermint leaves is a testament to (and vindication against) the obduracy of the lawn for once, and in their infancies, I near killed every single plant of them by not dead-heading the outgoing flowers come the end of the growing season and, but only for a November inspection which revealed to me the lignifications of bark creeping

60 Abbot Uisliu. He was forced to wave adieu
to the monastery due to unspecified dishonesties
and was last seen stumbling over London Bridge
(please see 'A Geologist's Fading Umbrage...')

along the length of each stem (their crawling and calciferous ossifications seeming to me, even then, a strange but timely mirroring off the cruel warping of bone onto cartilage that were waking inside Brother Fergus's knuckles) and so prompted me to immediately, and without mercy, cut each plant right back to its base, they all would have died and such timely intervention meant I was then able to nurse the bare stumps all through to the winter and into spring where, seeing the first new green shoots emerging from the stems of dry bark one morning I knew at last my vigil was over and my admonishment would stay, for one more year at least, with the grass alone,

the upward click of the black thumb-paddled switch tunes me back to the kettle, now in the final throes of its cluck-sputtering crescendo, and I am released at last because I know I now must go and pour the tea

turning away from the by now full-wettened windowpane, I tip the water in on top of the pyramidal teabag, a design much preferred by the Abbot as it increases the rate of convection (and thus, says he, transference of tea to water) and the stirring of my spoon swirls a tight vortex of clockwise current in the confines of the wide-handled mug, a mug that is, though chipped on the drinking side of the lip, still very much beloved to me being a gift from my mother on the day that she and my father came to watch me swear my vows

even now I remember unboxing it, her face watching mine as I took the white ceramic body out from amongst the nest of shredded paper and studied the detail of *hand in mosaic of Christ's death at the Church of the Holy Sepulchre* painted on its side

a single red spot on the sallow skin between second and third knuckle of the

right hand of Christ lying across a pale shroud
my mother's face watching me watching the mug

                                     and
not only was the heat of her adulation most warming
but I knew it would too weld, at last and for good, my
father again to her and her to him, for seeing her face in
that moment confirmed what I had long suspected – that
their pride in seeing me finally accepted to the order was
the final soldering stick needed to finish fusing together
their two naturally repellent poles (those being her
insular and stone-grey recalcitrance and his propensity
for angsting obsessions over the everyday and mundane)
and seeing them both stood so close that day and smiling
at me from across the cloister it was clear that they had
been proved right all along in their decision to lay down
their barbs and halberds all those years ago to unite
behind me because, here and in indisputable affirmation,
was their decision ratified and made both corpus and
flesh as they watched me now knelt low under the hand
of the Abbot

                   and they were aware too, of course, that
my swearing in would have the small (but not in-
consequential) bonus of allowing them to read my future
letters by the glow of the neighbour's envy

                             it is with the
blue-topped milk jug cocked over the steaming mug that
I hear the weasels moving again, some pale creatures of
yesteryear whose tip-tapping scrabbles have woken me
so often and woke me once more this morning, and their
scampering starts up anew and I feel them scuffle and flit
through my dusty eaves of memory, disturbing flakes
that float down through me

down through me even now as I'm stood watching
the milk cloud through the tea in tumults of teals and

yellowing-whites
                      motes falling down from my hidden
joists and settling themselves into shapes
                                  sometimes the
pattern on the mug
but most often forming themselves into the image of
that heaving murmuration of midges which clumped
low over myself and Deirdre that afternoon three days
before I joined the monastery, when we lay on the
shingled beach by the weir on our linen towels
     have you got a match for me
                              and I'd sat up and reached
over to fish the box from the pocket of my trousers,
coiled down as they were upon themselves in a flattened
disk beside my swimming bag, and I had lit one with a
sulphurous grind and held it behind the leeward cupping
of my hand
                the flaring green memory of her lighting her
cigarette floats across my eyes
                        and with her cigarette
finishing she had laid a hand on my elbow and asked if
I could teach her to swim – not knowing, of course,
that some days earlier I had watched her front crawl
effortlessly across of the weir; pushing back off the
wooden jetty and barely making a splash, her body
rolling a little with each stroke, her elbow pointing
skyward before the loose dangling arrangement of her
fingertips would trace a dappled dance of ripples across
the still face of the weir, ripples near indistinguishable
from those being made upstream by the top feeding
trout, before her extended arm would at last rotate at
the wrist and re-enter the water thumb-first and all the
while above me the midges massed in thick and angry
clouds

81

clasping two hands around the warmth of the mug,
I carry it back to the window in a bid that the weasels
be quiet, but my moving only sees them stir once
more and as the flakes settle anew I am again one of
nine walking up the gravel driveway toward the grey
limestone building and each of us is alight with the
embers of our own certainty, intent on burning the
world righteous,

        the numbers of the order back then
were forty-three so that it is hard to believe now there
are just six of us left

        no, only five, because just last week
the Abbot moved on Brother Cormac while the rest of
us slept, a missionary post in the Philippines he had told
us over that sinkhole of our breakfast

        and harder to
believe that *my* embers have now cooled, cooled so much
that it seems now more a clinker that rattles loose inside
— it was a clinker that beat out a hollow tattoo from
my chest when I watched Brother Conor finally lose
himself last month to his illustrated parchment on pre-
enlightenment studies of bats; that their brains were in
their feet or they were all small and clockwork demons
or really just robins pickled and leathered by darkness,
and so much time had he spent sketching this out on the
vellum rolls in his masterful and calligraphic script that,
in some kind of penance, he began to mutter opened-
mouthed along the corridors now more bat than man
and trying to echo-locate some insects of himself which
we must never hope to see,

        and it's a clinker I hear rattle
too every evening that Brother Duach comes home
shaking from all the abuse shouted at him through the
air-vent in the science lab (*The Freak* they call him, *Freak,
Freak, Freeeaaak*) and I ask every night that he might

learn to once again hang with sartorial elegance, that the students might just once, and for the love of the good man, listen, just listen,

and it's a clinker that rattles too when the Bishop[61] invites Brother Noisiu from Ghana up to the pulpit and I must pretend I don't hear the congregation sniggering louder and louder every week as Noisiu tells them once again about the power and mystery of *the say-crad hat of Jee-sos*

is that where my parents are now

both foetaled up together in that most mysterious hat somewhere and their pride in me still welding them together

and what about Deirdre, where is she now and does she still remember that she asked me to teach her to swim as the heat drove the midges thick down on us and the grass spoke in blazing rustles round our feet and does she now understand that it was the terrifying speed and incandescence of that moment at the weir that made me uncouple my trailer from the ball hitch of this world, made me unscrew whatever coupling bolt that was binding me to her and all else, lest the oscillations that were left tumbling and roiling through the rocky shelves of my chest after that day at the weir ever terrify me like that again, and would she understand now, even if I told her, how all that made me finally decide to put down my jockey wheel and trundle to a stop in the grey, limestone monastery house that sits thirteen miles outside Ballinteer and that every night since I've wondered did her happiness ever come to her and if it did was it wearing loose clothing

61 Who is now in Guatemala, of course.

> but as I sit on the red upholstered
armchair and make to drink my tea the pipes clink,
signalling Brother Fergus warming the water for his
shower and I see the sun is rising outside

> scared of the
dark again Ultan?

> at your age?
sure didn't the Abbot says that none of it matters now,
that isn't it all just the weasels again and that's just what
they do, dancing out their havoc up there, isn't it just
the racket they like to make but don't worry because he
knows I'll trap them bastards yet.

II: THE QUARREL OF THE TWO PIG KEEPERS[62]

Flagons and Rashers

Now Lushy Mac was – well he was a lush.
Not like Dackie Pa, the pissy auld mush
who you could near set the watch by because,
at half ten every morning *on the dot,*
you'd see him spindling out of Hartigan's
with three large flagons and a few bargain
packets of rashers. No, Lushy wasn't
anywhere as steady or as constant
as that. Since way back when, everyone in town
knew how it went with poor Lushy: head down
and, if you ever met him round the place,
he'd swear *blind,* swear straight your face,
that he was really done with drinking for good.
And he'd mean it too. But no sooner would
he finish adding the last waterproof solvent
to the new-built dam walls of his resolve
than a crack would appear. Nearly not there,
just a dark strand of hair, high-up somewhere
far off. But that'd be all it'd take.
The strand would become a spider's web, flake
off and widen, just a fraction to start,
and one tiny bead of longing would part
squeeze through, a bead *so small* that Lushy'd
not notice – but once that first drip of slushy

62 A brimstone-and-fire sermon,
on the consequences of fleshly and burning desire.
Unlike Mark, Lushy's
downfall is his gluttony
and tragic heroes like him are (as harsh as
it sounds) roasted on the pyres of their hamartia
in every small town up and down
the country.

want had returned then others, and so
the runny pangs for the porter would grow,
drip-filling the empty cistern of his brain
and he'd sail away on a bender again.

For the next week solid you'd see him stood,
stumbling outside of *The Bucket of Blood*,
that auld kip across from the dole office
where you're allowed leave half-finished
pints behind the bar to collect the next day,
and the whole week him wearing the same grey
and baize track suit, getting dirtier and
dirtier, and his pure tangly, tanned
head rolling around on his mankerous
shoulders and the terrible, cantankerous
murderings of *'The Auld Triangle'* only
baytin' hard out in his megaphony
voice. Well, only the first verse. You might think,
given Lushy'd been singing the same drink
soaked fucking song for twenty years
he would've learned the rest, but no fears
on that. But that, right there, was Lushy Mac.
Lushy'd only call a halt to it all
when he'd run out of money and be ball-
bag broke – but then it'd be way too late.
His job gone and, worse, his precarious fate
with Bernie (the poor long-suffering wife)
sealed – a black plastic bag with his life's
possessions thrown outside their wee house
down the bottom of the hill. Lushy'd grouch
the bag back to his poor soft-hearted Mam,
who was really too old for minding the man.

There he'd stay, holed up with the mother
for the next few days, and the smother

angsting maggots of his hangover
aytin' his brain and sweating him sober,
and then, like a drowned corpse,[63] he'd surface.
You'd see him hanging around by the cervix
of the road across from Bernie's, dressed
in his only suit, hair a Brylcream mess,
and Bernie in the door wearing her gown,
chain smoking fags with a scaldy frown
pretending she didn't know he was just
across the road with a bunch of crust
wilted flowers. But eventually
she'd relent, take him back. Essentially
everyone in town'd be delighted;
part because, somewhere deep down, they liked
Lushy, but most because it finally meant
an end to his mam moaning about rent
and, better, no more Lush moping about
with a head on him like a pint of gout.

But, over the months, the thirst'd drip back in
to the dusty crevices of his parchening
soul. And then, there'd he be for the week;
all of the blood vessels burst in his cheek,
wobbling about again outside *The Bucket*
roaring and everyone telling him *cut it
out*. That's just how it went. I'm not saying
he was a bad man really, sure weighing
it up he was just a poor shambolic
fool – but still an awful sceptic bollix.

87

63 Or a teacher's anger...

The Sow

One Friday last summer, Lush and The Sow
were heading home from work. Lushy'd somehow
wangled a job with Brophy — an extension
to the dole office and with the intention
being to save up enough to bring Bernie
on a pleasure cruise of Lough Erne. He
and The Sow were now strolling contently home,
on a type of evening that is well known
to workers; warm, bright and the possibility
of the weekend starting to crawl free
from the prison of the long evening shadows.
But outside *The Bucket* The Sow froze
dead, stuck in the syrups of laughter
oozing out through the broken plaster
and cracked panes of glass in the front door.
'Good be to the fucking Jesus,' he swore.
'I have the thirst of ten men on me here,'
and turned to the door, making to disappear.
The wafts of laughter escaped like hot air
outta an oven, blasting poor Lushy square
in the face. *'I nearly forgot,'* said The Sow,
and fished a brown envelope from down
in his pocket, stuffed with the week's
wages. He gave it to Lush, who squeaked
as he peered inside at the wad of
purple notes. The thick, sticky globs of
sweet and scented bank holiday laughter
were still tumbling on out one after
another. Lush looked down the street
toward Bernie's house, turned, looked back deep
into the pub. He wiped his brow with his sleeve.
The Sow, still in the doorway and bereaved
from waiting, nodded at Lush over his shoulder
'Up to you,' said the auld prick. *'Ah, no sure,'*

said Lush, *'it's the anniversary tonight,'*
'Nay bothers,' says The Sow, *'I'll see ya bright
and early Tuesday,'* and then he went in,
the haze of laughter enveloping him
away and out of sight. The door swung back,
muting the merriment and peals of craic
spilling out onto the street. *'Ah but just
one won't hurt,'* said Lushy, making a bust
inside before the door closed, muttering
'Ah, sure, one'll be grand.' And sure, just one
woulda been grand. Maybe even a couple
But it was the twelve that got him buckled.

The Sausage Supper

Drunks staggering out by the troop
and Lushy, in two loobawns and a hoop,
wobbling down the street, but enough sense
still to realise that vengeful recompense
would surely be paid if he dared return
to Bernie empty-handed and so, taciturn
with woe, but not ready to admit
defeat (meaning her going pure ape-shit)
he concocted an ingenious plan of attack:
a large sausage supper from *Wonder Macs*.
Then he pinballed home, the mangled strains
of *'The Auld Triangle'* leaking outta him again,
mumble mumble *'And a hungry feeling…'*
and the supper getting all cold. And eaten.

Outside home, Lush had a brain wave.
A creeping, teeth tingling and torturous crave
to empty his bladder had been pealing
through him like a bell,
                                        '…came o'er me stealing…'
and he decided that some quick relief
would help him avoid the aperitifs
of Bernie's anger as then he could billow
in, leaving the supper on her pillow
as a deft anniversary surprise,
before sneaking down and inside
the sheets like he'd never been out on the tear.
So, carefully down went the chips (quare
little of the sausage left) and, stumble,
'…and the mice were squealing… something mumble…'
he leaned his head on the wall, slow-trod
the legs out into a little tripod
and, so propped up, really concentrated
on directing the remains of the ill-fated

porter as far away from the supper
as he could.
                    '...And the auld triangle...'
Down went the zip.
                              '...went jingle-jangle...'
Out flopped his lad and Lushy let rip.
For near over two blissful minutes
he was as happy as only a thirsting
drunk who's been hammered and bursting
for a dirty slash can really understand:
'...along the banks of the Royal Canal!'
But wasn't Lushy forgetting something?
Sure he lived on a hill. And pumping
down the slope was a yellow and steaming
river of piss, one that was now streaming
all over the chips. And what was worse?
Hadn't the mangled strains of his cursed
singing only woken up Bernie, now leaning
out the doorway in the nightgown, her keening
eyes like murderous floodlights, as she watched
the sorry excuse for a poorly botched
shambles that was unfolding before her.
But Lush was not one to be deterred.
Over he staggered, picked up the chips
and offered them out to Bernie – the thick
trickles of warmth running over his cursory
gift.
    'Shere,' said he, *'Shappyshannyvershary.'*

III. THE WARP-SPASM

'Unexpected item in the bagging area,' says the only
working machine and you re-scan the bottle of Prosecco.
'Beep' and then you put the bottle into the bag beside
the expensive salsa and the corn chips. You usually buy
Economy. But not tonight. Because tonight you know
that someone special will be calling to the door of your
flat. In just over ten minutes. In your mind they are
already naked and – just for a sliver of time – they look
as good as only imaginary naked people can: no clear
discerning features, just a blur of perfect and exquisite
nakedness. But you wonder if thinking about them
naked will be like that day you arrived at work and
looked in your lunchbox, only to find your sandwich
was at home in the fridge. And for the rest of the day
you were unable to stop thinking about it and oh how
you had wanted that sandwich. But what if someone ate
it before you got back? Or what if, by the time you got
home, the tomato had sogged into the bread and ruined
it? After salivating over its tomatoey goodness all day it
would be hard to take and so maybe it would be better if
someone ate it after all and so, by degrees, you begin to
fear wanting that perfect and exquisite naked blur too
much and it too begins to resemble a large, if naked,
tomato sandwich. By now, behind your day-dreaming, a
queue has formed and it's getting longer by the minute.
A woman with a face like a barn owl is pretending to
wipe her glasses clean while really glowering at your
back. A man with an uncanny resemblance to a beagle is
holding a box of cornflakes and shuffling his feet. A few
places even further back and a vole-like chap is holding
the hand of his mousy daughter and muttering to his
ostrichy wife. 'Beep' goes the machine for the third time

and, in your haste to bag it up your hands become even clumsier than usual and the salsa rolls out of the bag. 'Unexpected item in the bagging area,' says the machine. *Not now* you think *not now not now not now* because to some of us there is simply nothing quite so beautiful as the knowledge that a moderately attractive office worker will soon ring our doorbell. And nothing quite so painful as the fear of not being there to answer. Confusion begins to tickle you with long and confusing fingers. Why is this bottle so unexpected? It is a bottle of Prosecco, a green one with a white and stylish label. This is a small supermarket, with a wine section. Surely the bottle should be the very thing a self-service machine in this supermarket would expect? Oh what a fool you were to dislike the surly shop assistant who used to work here, how you would welcome her gum-chewing disinterest now, how you would embrace her thinly-veiled contempt for the job. Clean goes the owl. Stare goes the beagle. Mutter goes the vole.
Comeoncomeoncomeon you say with a whole disapproving Farthing Wood behind you, before adding *Please*. You have been raised to be polite, even to obdurate electronic equipment. *What is that person saying?* says Beagle Features. *I'm not sure,* replies Barn Owl, *Something about cheese I think. I wish they'd hurry up.* Beagle Features groans. *Cheese? As well?* Says Vole and not muttering any more, *We'll be here all bloody day. I wish they'd stop talking to the machine and bloody buy something.* 'Beep' goes the Prosecco again. 'Unexpected item,' says the machine. *I know I know,* you begin to say, but the machine adds 'in the bagging area,' anyway. Try as you might, you just cannot fathom the depths of the bottle's unexpectedness – although it is beginning to feel as if you have swum down in an attempt to do so and are now fast running out of air. In place of confusion's fingers go now the

pinchy digits of frustration in the face of perceived
electronic injustice. Pinch go the fingers. Pinch pinch
pinch. You bang your forehead on the machine top.
Look, says Owl Face, *They can't do that, can they? Yes,* says
Beagle Features, *Where's their decency?* and he shakes his
head in disgust. You are pretending not to hear them,
but you cannot ignore their eyeballs devouring the back
of your neck. You know how they see you. They see
you as a crook, as a thief. These are not just any old
people you are holding up, they are *individuals.* They are
all individuals, with hopes and dreams and places to be
and aspirations that cannot be realised whilst they are
stuck in this queue. Who are you to take their dreams
away from them? Do you think they are people who can
afford to idle away their days in supermarket queues?
They work hard. They pay their taxes. They don't
deserve this. They most certainly do not deserve this.
The hairs on their necks bristle and the queue became a
tinderbox – resting on a knife edge. And all the while
your watch ticks and the pinchy digits pinch on. You
move the corn chips to *absolutely* make sure that there is
enough room in the bag for the Prosecco. Then you scan
the bottle one more time. 'Beep,' says the machine. You
place the bottle into the bag and held your breathe. Tick.
Tock. The machine is silent. Tick. Tock. And then it says
… 'Unexpected item in the bagging area.' Your anger
froths out like milk boiling over. [64] White rolls of rage
bubble down you and puddled on the floor. You begin
to beat the machine, swinging the packet of corn chips in
wide and swathing arcs. *You cretinous mechanical moron!*
you scream, *It's not a naked mole rat!* In your anger you
have forgotten that naked mole rats are neither really rats
or moles but are actually a sub-species of porcupine.
Maybe if you had remembered this, things would have
worked out differently. *It's a bottle of wine!* you shout, *and*

94

63 Again? Alpha to omega.

this is a supermarket! I've scanned it five fucking times! The machine blinks at you, pretending not to understand but its silence only enrages you further. You begin to thrash the machine with a renewed vigour. The packet of corn chips bursts open due to the ferocity of the beating and triangular snacks go cartwheeling through the air. A spinning chip spears the owl-faced woman on the earlobe and she begins to tremor on the spot – very quietly at first, like an electric toothbrush that has fallen into a sock drawer and accidentally switched itself on. But when a second starchy triangle hits her on the chin she explodes. *Assault! Assault on that that poor machine! Swearing and assaulting that machine, that innocent machine! Isn't someone going to do something?* Righteous and owlish indignation shoots out of her and into the air like matches being flicked into a field of dry grass. They rain down on the rest of the shoppers who explode, one by one, and go careening around the supermarket. *The children, think of the children,* wails the ostrichy woman and she covers her daughter's mousy eyes. *Oh my god, will you have some self-respect,* barks Beagle Features, shamed into action by Owl Face's outburst and his thin walls of stoicism now tumbling down. He bites chunks out of his cornflakes box and begins to spit out mouthfuls of cardboard. *Pull yourself together,* he says, *you're embarrassing yourself. You're embarrassing all of us.* A teenager who has been trying to buy a donut for the last twenty minutes shoots back off into the bakery section and begins to dismantle the shelving. A granddad with beady mole-eyes (who had only come in to buy some breakfast biscuits) is carried along by the waves of mind-warping fury now sweeping through the supermarket. Being toward the back of the queue he does not fully understand what is happening – but he knows he doesn't like it. He has not fought in a world war for this, definitely not for this, and so he begins to beat his walking stick on the floor. Unusually large tears began to roll out of his eyes and you might not think that a man with such small and moley eyes could produce such large tears but he can. You, however, are now encased in a hardening skin of gibbering insanity. You are now saying things that have no real meaning, like the barcode of an onion remember from your lowly days working in *Roots 'n' Fruits. 36220000440,* you say, your mind no longer your own. A librarian with a fully loaded basket has become unhinged by the slowness of the queue and is now sat cross legged on the floor, immolating herself with the contents of her basket; custard, treacle, mayonnaise, pilchards, crème fraîche. She had only come in because of a hankering for carrot batons but had then filled her basket with things she never usually bought, things she didn't even particularly like. What a terrible day to fill her basket with such slimy produce. What rotten luck. The packet of corn chips is now completely empty but you are still thrashing the machine for all you are worth. *36220000440,* you say. 'Unexpected item in the bagging area,' says the machine and you know that right now, at this very moment, someone is ringing your buzzer. You see their index finger pressing the button and hear the buzzing echoing through the empty depths of your flat. Or rather, you would if your mind was your own. But it is not, it has left you like innocence leaving a bukkake. You open the salsa and begin flagellating yourself with it. You apply it to your face like make-up. You fill your pockets with it. You throw it in the air like wet and gooey confetti. You are no longer human, you are but a warbling barcode automaton, a salsa-smeared robot of despair. 'Unexpected item in the bagging area,' says the machine and by now the crowd is rabid. Queue-related hatreds have burst forth from their ids and are flying around the shop like ghosts escaped from inter-dimensional portals. All the occasions that they had stood in lines only to be gazumped have come flooding back; the memories of times when, after waiting so patiently, their counter had closed and another one had opened. They recall, aghast, how everyone behind them had then run to the newly opened counter pretending to be innocent of what they are doing and the shoppers start to bay like coyotes, coyotes who wanted blood of those who cannot queue, who will not queue, those who think it O.K. to steal other people's precious time. So when you say *36220000440* again but still do not pay for anything it is simply too much. The owl-faced woman punches you right on the ear and down you go like a teenager's zip. But the crowd cannot be sated so easily, no more than you could be saved from a lion by throwing it a lettuce and they fall upon your un-moving body with the fervour of peasants discovering the same potato during the famine. They tear into you. Beagle Features stabs you repeatedly with the keys of his cripplingly expensive house. The ostrichy woman skewers one of your eyeballs with her stiletto, shoes she wears for work not because they were comfortable but because not to do so would have hurt her career prospects. The mole-eyed granddad pulls on your left arm until it comes off and then swings it around his head. The voleish chap, releasing years of pent up suffering at the hands of his overbearing wife, bites off your nose. Children ransack your body. They dig through your abdomen with their little fingers, tearing out your organs and then squawking as they hold your innards up to the fluorescent lights. You must never let someone steal your time; they seem to say with each fresh assault, never, never, never. Eventually, when bits of you have been scattered cathartically all through the supermarket, the crowd begins to abate. Blood-spattered shoppers forget what they had been doing. They pick themselves up, exchanging glances as might a man and his neighbour's wife upon discovering each other in a pornography emporium. One by one, and without speaking, they begin to leave. Men scuttle out the side exits and into the plaza, keeping their eyes on the floor. Women pretend to put on their make-up before following suit. Parents grab their children, adjusting their little collars and wiping slimy entrail residue away from their faces. Then they leave through the front and go off about their business – and all the while the machine sings on. 'Unexpected item,' it sings. 'Unexpected item in the bagging area.'

All Denizens (Real & Imagined)

Acknowledgements

The room is dark, the pipes are cooling
as I write these final words,
and each one fills me with a pooling
sense of luck – I have an absurd
number of most helpful supporters,
without whom the first bricks, mortars
(and then cornicing) of this book
would not exist – or at least look
anything like they do. So, to Ardu
and Jack (tutors both first rate),
Brendan and Ken (feedback great)
Andrew and Jack B. (critics who
most honest speak) Rosie, Todd S. –
for all your help I've been blessed;

and thank you (and indeed most kindly)
to the following magazines,
where these poems (or some blindly
wrought prior attempts) first dreamed;
breathed: *Ink Sweat And Tears, Three Drops
From A Cauldron, Magma, The Runt*, lots
posted in *The Galway Review,
Silver Apples* mag, *The Best New
British And Irish Anthology*
(twice)*, The Irish Lit Times*,
Dodging The Rain (all un-rhymed),
Bare Fiction and *Southbank Poetry,
The Blythe Hill*. For airing my work:
most hearty thanks – from S. N. Bourke.

A Brief And Final Note

Loads of poets are out there poeting,
even now, now, this very now,
performing and putting Stoic ink
to paper, so here's (and in no
particular order) a smallish
(very smallish), list of polished
performers out there writing great,
really exciting, and weight
-y, innovative stuff. It's by no
means exhaustive – just a few
writers I've been lucky enough to
read – or read with – or see their shows.
So why not aim to go beserk
On the following's handiwork?

Chrissy Williams, Robert Cole, Jericho Brown, AK Blakemore,
Maria Apichella, Harriet Creelman, Aisling Fahey, Belinda
Zahawi, Mark Waldron, Susannah Dickey, Joshua Seigel
Conor Cleary, Toby Buckley (curator of the exzzzellent zine
called Bombinate), Jackie Gorman, Chelsea Minnis, Jennifer L
Knox, Jenna Clake, Tara Skurtu, Christian Wethered, Victoria
Kennefick, Sarah Perry, Jack Underwood, Emily Berry, Kaveh
Akbar, Grace Wilentz, Majella Kelly, Colin Dardis, Kevin
Bateman, Theo Dorgan, Colette Bryce, Lucreta from Brockley,
Bartle Sawbridge, Ciara Ní É, Scroobius Pip, Stephen Sexton,
Aoife Bourke, Jodie Porter, Breda Spaight, James O'Leary, Mathew
Rice, Luke Kennard, Andrew McWhirter, Sinéad Morrisey, Dean
Atta, Paul Durcan, Tomas Tranströmer, Wayne Holloway Smith,
Raymond Antrobus, Anthony Anaxagorou, Anne Casey, James
O'Leary, Darren Donoghue, Paul Ó Colmáin, Katherine Kilalea,
Oliver Jones, The Blythe Hill Tavern Poetry Night run by Mike
McKenna, Oliver from Germany, Joshua Osto, Abiola Oni, Bartle
Sawbridge, Jake Kirner, Kerri O'Brien, Rosanna Hildyard, Todd
Swift, Toni Stuart, Michael Naughton Shanks, Clifton Redmond,
Captain Moonlight, Lotti Dingle, Cherry Potts.

EYEWEAR PUBLISHING